Twenty-five Years of Exploration in

Wyoming's Red Desert

Photography by Paul Ng

Foreword by Charlie Love

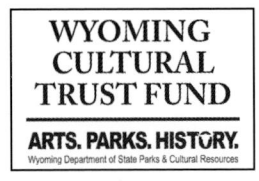

"Supported in part by a grant from the Wyoming Cultural Trust Fund,
a program of the Department of State Parks and Cultural Resources."
And, sponsored by Sweetwater Board of Cooperative Educational Services.

ISBN 10: 1-59152-136-X
ISBN 13: 978-1-59152-136-5

Published by Board of Cooperative Educational Services (BOCES)

Photography © 2014 by Paul Ng

All rights reserved. This book may not be reproduced in whole or in part by any means
(with the exception of short quotes for the purpose of review) without the permission of the publisher.

For more information, write Paul Ng, 3204 Fir Drive, Rock Springs, WY 82901
www.paulngphotography.com

sweetgrassbooks
a division of Farcountry Press

Produced by Sweetgrass Books; PO Box 5630, Helena, MT 59604;
(800) 821-3874; www.sweetgrassbooks.com.

Printed in China.

17 16 15 14   1 2 3 4 5 6 7

To My Wonderful Wife and Lovely Daughter

Betty and Jessica

and the memory of my parents

Kai Min and Yuk Ling

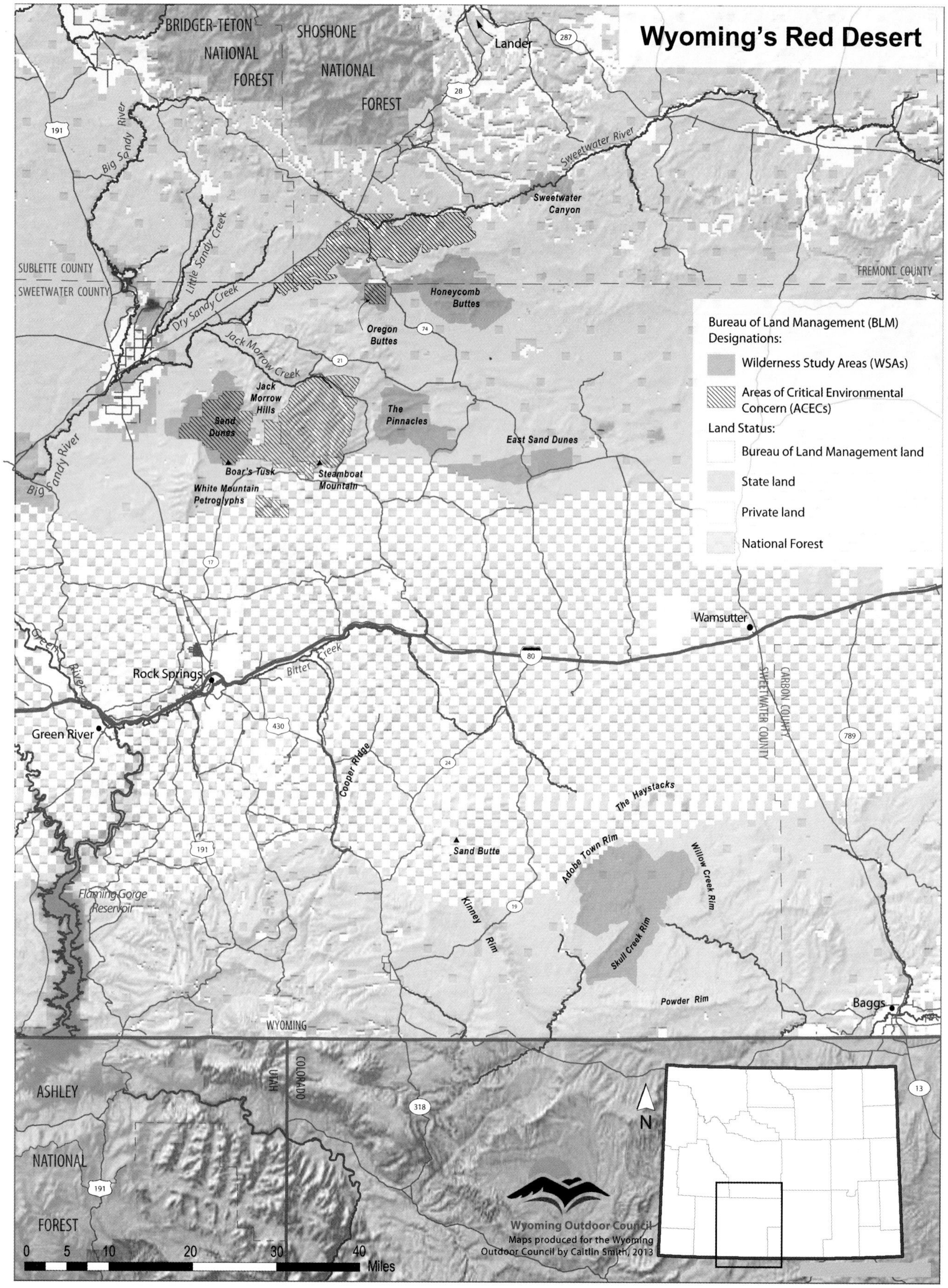

Wyoming's Red Desert
BRIDGER-TETON NATIONAL FOREST
SHOSHONE NATIONAL FOREST
Lander
Sweetwater River
Sweetwater Canyon
Big Sandy River
Little Sandy Creek
Dry Sandy Creek
Jack Morrow Creek
SUBLETTE COUNTY
SWEETWATER COUNTY
FREMONT COUNTY
Honeycomb Buttes
Oregon Buttes
Jack Morrow Hills
Sand Dunes
The Pinnacles
East Sand Dunes
Boar's Tusk
Steamboat Mountain
White Mountain Petroglyphs
Bureau of Land Management (BLM) Designations:
Wilderness Study Areas (WSAs)
Areas of Critical Environmental Concern (ACECs)
Land Status:
Bureau of Land Management land
State land
Private land
National Forest
Wamsutter
Rock Springs
Green River
Bitter Creek
CARBON COUNTY
SWEETWATER COUNTY
Cooper Ridge
The Haystacks
Adobe Town Rim
Willow Creek Rim
Sand Butte
Kinney Rim
Skull Creek Rim
Powder Rim
Flaming Gorge Reservoir
Baggs
WYOMING
UTAH
COLORADO
ASHLEY NATIONAL FOREST
N
Wyoming Outdoor Council
Maps produced for the Wyoming Outdoor Council by Caitlin Smith, 2013
0 5 10 20 30 40 Miles

Foreword

Anyone I've met who has traveled in any part of a somewhat vague area that is called the Red Desert of southwest Wyoming, has developed both mental and emotional images about what they experienced. The discussions between people who have been "there" always seems to produce a colorful patchwork quilt of what the region has to offer and usually it includes some mention of scientific discoveries, observations on wildlife, geology, archaeology, fossils, history, adventure and even myth they selflessly make up just for you. The photos that Paul Ng offers in this book illustrate different fractions of all of these. The Red Desert is myth, and can't be confined by lines drawn on a map.

When you are standing on top of Steamboat Mountain, the view of the seemingly endless great divide basin out to the east in the late afternoon is overwhelming. Pastel yellows and browns and pinks and occasionally dark green paint the landscape. And when you look around and down you not only see the march of enormous parabolic sand dunes for 70 miles, but the remains of a prehistoric buffalo jump, a estimonial to the close environmental adaptation that Native Americans had for thousands of years. You have a feeling in this wondrous enormity of space just how big and uninhabited it is, and just how tiny and inconspicuous we are. It is home to all forms of wildlife that roam in this area, which is the size of Massachusetts, Connecticut, and Rhode Island combined. It contains the entire Great Divide Basin, the largest internal drainage system in all of North America.

To the committed observer, however, at least four major factors go into what the Red Desert is. The bedrock geology is only the first layer in view because it doesn't change as much as the human interpretation of it. The geology is covered with a veneer of vegetation which in turn is controlled by climate and results in numerous unique species. In spite of only 5-7 inches of rain and snow over much of the region, this area is home to many small ponds & lakes that sustain other unusual species, such as salamanders. The Red Desert also straddles the fly ways of many different birds and few of those migrants stay very long.

The dominant public interest tends to be in the nature of wild places, but even this is a sliding scale. The view and interest of the rancher is very different than the view of the federal land management agencies, and they view it differently than the fish & wildlife agencies. Scientists and academic folks have still other viewpoints, all of which illustrate the diversity and balance the bedrock has created. However one defines it.

So there is the physical reality embodied in the rocks. From our viewpoint on Steamboat Mountain there is an economic reality that is reflected in the oil & gas development and their well locations, pipelines and access roads are ubiquitous. Off to the east you can see steam rising from the Jim Bridger power plant cooling towers, fueled by low sulfur coal deposits, which allows electric power to flow to folks in Idaho & Oregon. On a clear chill day looking off to the west in the early morning, steam rises from the cooling ponds of the 4 major trona mines and processing buildings. They are only 40 miles away beyond Pilot Butte, busy producing train loads of sodium bi-carbonate intrinsic in making glass, perfume, soap, deodorant and cat litter and a little box for your refrigerator—so that your leftover decaying food doesn't smell quite so bad.

But the rancher and his need for irrigation water and pasturage sees the land and what water there is very differently, as do the people trying to protect eagles and wild horses. Sprinkled throughout the dunes are numerous little bands of wild horses and antelope. Rain and winter snow melt seep down through the dunes, pool on an impermeable clay layer and allows the ponds to sustain complex ecosystems. The Red Desert is so prolific in sustaining wild life and sheep & cattle, that it maintains explorations for oil & gas, and coal & trona. There are so many kinds of explorations that they too are required to sustain the wild life—including eagles and sage grouse on smaller and smaller patches of ground. The desert is at an interesting cross roads to see how long industry can sustain their development along with sustaining the islands of wildlife. Many of Paul Ng's photos, most of which are not published here, can be among the "before" pictures of this century.

And finally there is the dramatic prehistoric side of the Red Desert, including ten or eleven thousand years worth of Indian history, the gradual arrival of whites, cavalry and railroads, and finally ranches and bone hunters, and the automobile and finally the most unpredictable creature of all: the tourist. Paul Ng's photos contain all of the changing roles the human side of the Red Desert country can provide.

As the nation's population grows, more and more pressure will be placed on development of open land, spaces like the Red Desert and will be continuously eaten away bit by bit. Eventually Paul Ng's book will be moved from the art or social science area of libraries, and be placed in the history section. We know, for example, that the mammoths became extinct between 9,000 and 11,000 years ago and that the 800 lbs of vegetation daily needed to keep these behemoths alive, has disappeared completely. Finding butchered skeletons of mammoths in the other basins of Wyoming, a few fragments of teeth and polished chunks of ivory attest to their presence in this section of Wyoming. Elsewhere in Wyoming skeletons of the largest lions and cheetahs ever known give evidence as to why the modern antelope can run so fast. Arctic muskox have been found preserved in an area just north east of the Green River Basin. All of these have disappeared and only diminutive forms remain.

Like Yellowstone National Park, which began as a geologic park in 1872, and has now morphed into a wildlife park in only 100 years, the Red Desert will become a remaining open space. In 1872 there were lots of buffalo, elk, deer, bighorn sheep, and antelope outside of the park boundaries. Now, none of those animals are safe outside the park boundaries. The Red Desert is changing in a very similar fashion because of the comparative isolation of the region. But because there are rigid limitations regarding resource extraction in Yellowstone, we all will see what the difference another 50 years will make in the comparatively untrammeled use of the Red Desert.

Charlie Love
2013

The Red Desert Through My Camera Lens

Wyoming's Red Desert is a pristine landscape but not many people know about it and less number of people venture into the area. It is far less popular than Yellowstone and the Grand Teton. The Red Desert provides plenty of opportunities for outdoor recreation, hunting, hiking, camping and photography. The Red Desert is also a prime habitat for a large herd of desert elk in the country. Thousands of wild horses roam freely in the Red Desert. The size of this vast BLM-managed area is in the neighborhood of 9,400 square miles.

When I first moved from the green hills of Tennessee to Rock Springs, Wyoming in 1980, I was in shock to see this vast barren land with hardly any trees other than scrubs like sagebrush and greasewood. It took me years to discover the beauty of the unique rock formations and the sand dunes in the area. When I first ventured into Killpecker Sand Dunes with a camera in 1988, I came back with my first memorable image of the sand dunes with fence. In fact, I got so carried away that I photographed until dark. I almost could not find my way back to the car. From that day on, I kept going back to the dunes almost every year and sometimes several times a year, always with a camera. When I started making black and white images with a 4X5 large format camera in 1991, I began to expand my journeys into other areas of the Red Desert; including Pine Canyon, White Mountain Petroglyphs, Plume Rock, Honeycomb Buttes, Oregon Buttes and many other spots in the area. In October, 2003, I finally made my first photographic trip to Adobe Town Rim. For the last ten years, I have made more than a few dozen trips to Adobe Town and Skull Creek Rim areas. There are hundreds of rock formations in these sites. Quite often I photographed the same rock site more than a few times because they looked different from various angles and under different lighting.

I am fortunate to live within a hundred miles from most of these areas that I have photographed during the past twenty-five years. Undoubtedly some of the best images that I ever made are from the Red Desert of Wyoming.

Unfortunately, the area is ever changing due to erosion and other natural and man-made factors. To preserve today's images of the region, one of the most feasible forms of documentations is to capture these pristine landscapes on film, and my choice is by a 4X5 large format camera with black and white film.

Paul Ng
Rock Springs, Wyoming
November, 2013

PLATE 1: Fence, Killpecker Sand Dunes at Dusk. The first image ever made in Killpecker Sand Dunes in 1988.

PLATE 2: Shadows and waves, Killpecker Sand Dunes

PLATE 3: Shadows and patterns, Killpecker Sand Dunes

PLATE 4: Sand hill number one, Killpecker Sand Dunes

PLATE 5: Sand dunes on a calm late afternoon

PLATE 6: Crest and hills, Killpecker Sand Dunes

PLATE 7: Sand hill number two, Killpecker Sand Dunes

PLATE 8: Winter moonrise at Killpecker Sand Dunes

PLATE 9: Late afternoon clouds at Killpecker Sand Dunes

PLATE 10: Wind-sculpted sand table, Killpecker Sand Dunes

PLATE 11: Wind-sculpted sand castle, Killpecker Sand Dunes

PLATE 12: Moonrise over Steamboat Mountains and Killpecker Sand Dunes

PLATE 13: Windy afternoon at Killpecker Sand Dunes

PLATE 14: Wind and snow sculpted slabs, Killpecker Sand Dunes

PLATE 15: Sand patterns in the winter, Killpecker Sand Dunes

PLATE 16: Sand blocks and canyon carved by wind and snow in the winter, Killpecker Sand Dunes

PLATE 17: Sand hills and layers, Killpecker Sand Dunes

PLATE 18: Early summer wildflower blossom, Killpecker Sand Dunes

PLATE 19: Sand hill in the middle of winter, Killpecker Sand Dunes

PLATE 20: Sand Dunes Wilderness Study Area, White Mountains in the distance

PLATE 21: Sand pancakes, Killpecker Sand Dunes

PLATE 22: Boar's Tusk, near Killpecker Sand Dunes

PLATE 23: Rock Garden, Pine Canyon

PLATE 24: Charred trees, Castle Rock, Pine Canyon

PLATE 25: Peculiar rock formations, White Mountain Petroglyphs

PLATE 26: Storm clouds over North Table Mountain

PLATE 27: Plume Rock, along the Oregon Trail near Oregon Buttes

PLATE 28: North Oregon Butte (right) and South Oregon Butte (left) in early morning

PLATE 29: Sunrise, Oregon Buttes in northern Sweetwater County

PLATE 30: Sunset, Honeycomb Buttes, Sweetwater County

PLATE 31: A pyramid-shaped butte in Honeycomb Buttes

PLATE 32: Honeycomb Buttes in early morning, Continental Peak in the distance

PLATE 33: Pulpit Rock, south of Interstate Highway 80 between Green River and Rock Springs

PLATE 34: Back-lit Pilot Butte, on top of White Mountain north of Rock Springs

PLATE 35: Badland east of Rock Springs

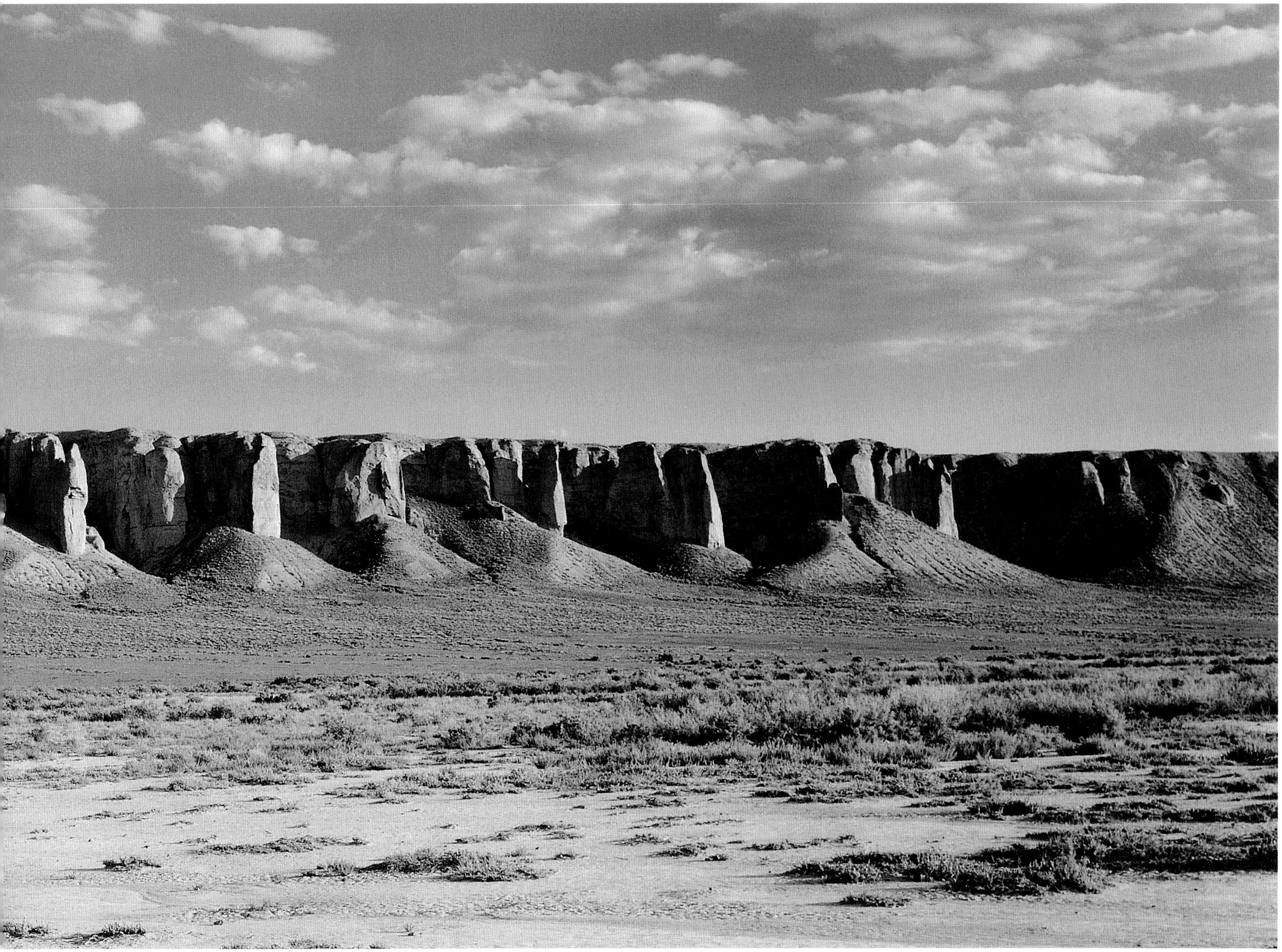

PLATE 36: Moon over rock formations near Point of Rocks

PLATE 37: Rock cropping west of Point of Rocks, Sweetwater County

PLATE 38: Petroglyphs near Point of Rocks, Sweetwater County

PLATE 39: A night view of Jim Bridger Powerplant near Point of Rocks

PLATE 40: Carmel Rock, south of Rock Springs, Sweetwater County

PLATE 41: Ferris Mountains, unofficially the northeast boundary of the Red Desert, Carbon County

PLATE 42: Rock pinnacles at sunset, Adobe Town Rim, Sweetwater County

PLATE 43: Tower Rock number one, Adobe Town Rim, Sweetwater County

PLATE 44: Plenty of rock formations like these in Adobe Town

PLATE 45: Cracked mud patterns, Adobe Town

PLATE 46: Tower Rock number one, brain-shaped boulder, Adobe Town

PLATE 47: Rock formation, Lower Valley, Adobe Town

plate 48: Tower Rock number two, Adobe Town Rim

PLATE 49: Castle Rock, Adobe Town Rim

PLATE 50: Tower Rock number two before sun down, Adobe Town Rim

PLATE 51: Mexican Hat Valley, Adobe Town Rim

PLATE 52: Looking beyond the stone forest in Adobe Town Rim

PLATE 53: Rock columns, Adobe Town

PLATE 54: Boulder trapped between two rock columns, Adobe Town

PLATE 55: Dried mud patterns at a wash, Adobe Town

PLATE 56: Rolling stones in a dry wash, Adobe Town

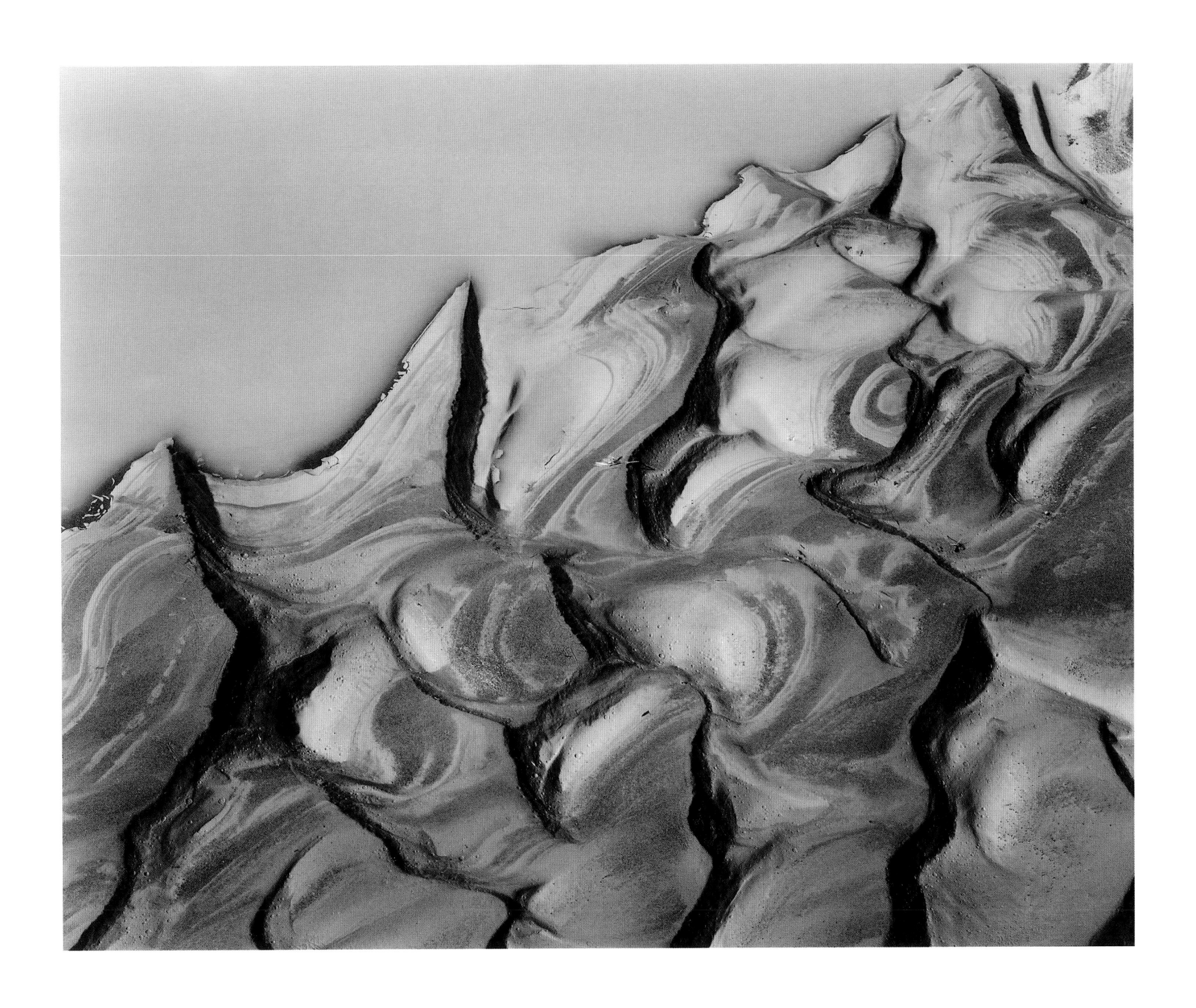

PLATE 57: Mud patterns, Adobe Town Rim

PLATE 58: Rock columns and pinnacles, Adobe Town

PLATE 59: Living room of an old ranch house, near Skull Creek Rim

PLATE 60: Tower Rock number three, Adobe Town Rim

PLATE 61: Spring run-off, below the Adobe Town Rim

PLATE 62: Hole in the rock wall, Adobe Town

PLATE 63: The Haystacks south of Wamsutter, Sweetwater County

PLATE 64: Family of three, wild horses, iconic in the Red Desert

PLATE 65: Skull Creek Rim over-look, Sweetwater County

List of Plates

Plate 1 — Fence, Killpecker Sand Dunes at dusk, first image ever made in Killpecker Sand Dunes, 1988
Plate 2 — Shadows and waves, Killpecker Sand Dunes, 1999
Plate 3 — Shadows and patterns, Killpecker Sand Dunes, 1997
Plate 4 — Sand hill number one, Killpecker Sand Dunes, 2005
Plate 5 — Sand dunes on a calm late afternoon, 1992
Plate 6 — Crest and hills, Killpecker Sand Dunes, 2007
Plate 7 — Sand hill number two, Killpecker Sand Dunes, 2007
Plate 8 — Winter moonrise, Killpecker Sand Dunes, 2001
Plate 9 — Late afternoon clouds, Killpecker Sand Dunes, 2004
Plate 10 — Wind-sculpted sand table, Killpecker Sand Dunes, 2004
Plate 11 — Wind-sculpted sand castle, Killpecker Sand Dunes, 2004
Plate 12 — Moonrise over Steamboat Mountains and Killpecker Sand Dunes, 2006
Plate 13 — Windy afternoon at Killpecker Sand Dunes, 2008
Plate 14 — Wind and snow sculpted slabs, Killpecker Sand Dunes, 2010
Plate 15 — Sand patterns in the winter, Killpecker Sand Dunes, 2012
Plate 16 — Sand blocks and canyon carved by wind and snow in the winter, Killpecker Sand Dunes, 2004
Plate 17 — Sand hills and layers, Killpecker Sand Dunes, 2009
Plate 18 — Early summer wildflower blossom, Killpecker Sand Dunes, 1999
Plate 19 — Sand hill in the middle of winter, Killpecker Sand Dunes, 2001
Plate 20 — Sand Dunes Wilderness Study Area, White Mountain in the distance, 2013
Plate 21 — Sand pancakes, Killpeclker Sand Dunes, 2009
Plate 22 — Boar's Tusk, near Killpecker Sand Dunes, 1998
Plate 23 — Rock Garden, Pine Canyon, 2004
Plate 24 — Charred trees, Castle Rock, Pine Canyon, 2008
Plate 25 — Peculiar rock formations, White Mountain Petroglyphs, 1998
Plate 26 — Storm clouds over North Table Mountain, 1997
Plate 27 — Plume Rock, along the Oregon Trail near Oregon Buttes, 2006
Plate 28 — North Oregon Butte (right) and South Oregon Butte (left) in early morning, 2013
Plate 29 — Sunrise, Oregon Buttes in northern Sweetwater County, 2013
Plate 30 — Sunset, Honeycomb Buttes, Sweetwater County, 2013
Plate 31 — A pyramid-shaped butte in Honeycomb Buttes, 2011
Plate 32 — Honeycomb Buttes in early morning, Continental Peak in the distance, 2013
Plate 33 — Pulpit Rock, south of Interstate Highway 80 between Green River and Rock Springs, 1998

Plate 34 — Back-lit Pilot Butte, on top of White Mountain north of Rock Springs, 2013
Plate 35 — Badland east of Rock Springs, 2003
Plate 36 — Moon over rock formations near Point of Rocks, 1995
Plate 37 — Rock cropping west of Point of Rocks, 1995
Plate 38 — Petroglyphs near Point of Rocks, Sweetwater County, 2013
Plate 39 — A night view of Jim Bridger Power Plant near Point of Rocks, 2007
Plate 40 — Carmel Rock, south of Rock Springs, Sweetwater County, 1998
Plate 41 — Ferris Mountains, unofficially the north-eastern boundary of the Red Desert, Carbon County, 2013
Plate 42 — Rock pinnacles at sunset, Adobe Town Rim, Sweetwater County, 2003
Plate 43 — Tower Rock number one, Adobe Town Sweetwater County, 2003
Plate 44 — Plenty of rock formations like these in Adobe Town, 1997
Plate 45 — Cracked mud patterns, Adobe Town, 2005
Plate 46 — Tower Rock number one, brain-shaped boulder, Adobe Town, 2008
Plate 47 — Rock formation, Lower Valley, Adobe Town, 2009
Plate 48 — Tower Rock number two, Adobe Town, 2008
Plate 49 — Castle Rock, Adobe Town, 2005
Plate 50 — Tower Rock number two before sun down, Adobe Town Rim, 2009
Plate 51 — Mexican Hat Valley, Adobe Town Rim, 2009
Plate 52 — Looking beyond the stone forest in Adobe Town Rim, 2008
Plate 53 — Rock columns, Adobe Town, 2013
Plate 54 — Boulder trapped between two rock columns, Adobe Town, 2010
Plate 55 — Dried mud patterns at a wash, Adobe Town, 2010
Plate 56 — Rolling stones in a dry wash, Adobe Town, 2010
Plate 57 — Mud patterns, Adobe Town, 2010
Plate 58 — Rock columns and pinnacles, Adobe Town, 2012
Plate 59 — Living room of an old ranch house, near Skull Creek Rim, 2010
Plate 60 — Tower Rock number three, Adobe Town Rim, 2008
Plate 61 — Spring run-off, below Adobe Town Rim, 2012
Plate 62 — Hole in the rock wall, Adobe Town, 2012
Plate 63 — The Haystacks south of Wamsutter, Sweetwater County, 2012
Plate 64 — Family of three, wild horses, iconic in the Red Desert, 2013
Plate 65 — Skull Creek Rim over-look, Sweetwater County, 2013

A few words on my photographs

On numerous occasions, friends, students and strangers have asked me what photographic gear and film I use. Therefore, I assume some readers of this book would raise similar questions.

All but three of the images in this book were captured with a 4X5 large format camera. I used either a Wista DX Rosewood 4X5 field camera or a Linhof Master Techika 2000, with lens of various focal lengths including 75mm, 90mm, 150mm, 210mm and 300mm. Several tripods have been used over the years, including Slik, Benro, Gitzo and Manfrotto. The first image of "Fence, Killpecker Sand Dunes at Dusk" was made using Kodak TMax 100 film with a Leica 35mm camera and a 35mm wide-angle lens. The image of "Family of Three, Wild Horses, Iconic in the Red Desert" was made with a Nikon N90s and a 300mm lens with Kodak Tri-X 400 film. The photograph of "Sand Dunes on a Calm Late Afternoon" was captured with a Hasselblad 500CM medium format camera with Ilford film. My choices of 4X5 sheet film are Kodak TMax ISO 100 and 400, and Kodak Tri-X ISO 320.

I process all the film myself as soon I get home, usually with Kodak D-76 film developer and occasionally with PMK developer. I hand print from selected negatives using a Saunders/LPL 4500II enlarger with color head or a VCCE module and Nikkor EL lens. In the darkroom process, I may employ basic techniques such as dodging and burning, split filtration printing, and use of an unsharp mask on occasion. Bleaching is often a technique that I use in adjusting densities in shadow areas. All the prints for this book project were processed in Kodak Dektol print developer and selenium-toned. My choices of enlarging papers are Ilford Multigrade Fiber-based or Oriental Variable Contrast FB paper.

Large format black and white is my domain in photography, but I have photographed with transparencies. I used to make Cibachrome (later called Ilfochrome) prints from time to time. In recent years, I have been experimenting in digital photography. However, my love in photography is still in the dark room.

All photographs for this book project were drum-scanned from original handmade prints.

Paul Ng

Acknowledgments

Images from twenty-five years' collection cannot be easily reproduced into a photo book without major collaborations with different entities and help from many individuals. I would like to take this opportunity to express my gratitude to a few friends and professionals who rendered help along the process.

This book project would not be possible without the sponsorships from Sweetwater County Board of Cooperative Educational Services and the Wyoming Cultural Trust Fund. My sincere thanks go to Dr. Bernadine Craft, Director of SBOCES and Theresa Piaia, secretary at the BOCES office; and also to their board members including Dick Boettcher, Robert Ramsey, Ann Rudoff, Brady Baldwin, Cristy McBee and Shannon Honaker.

Renee Boveé, Administrator of Wyoming Cultural Trust Fund, provided plenty of valuable information in grant application. It was a great opportunity to meet the board members of Wyoming Cultural Trust Fund: Nancy Schiffer, Jim Davis, Dave Kathka, Susan Stubson and Sara Needles when they held the meeting for grant reviews in Rock Springs in the spring of 2013. I am grateful for their support.

I am indebted to Charlie Love for taking his time to write the foreword for this book. His wealth of knowledge in every aspect in geology, archaeology and history is extremely valuable and educational.

My special thanks go to Ed Varley, John and Debbie Eversole, for their advice and directions in getting around the maze of Adobe Town.

Kudos to Julia Stuble of Wyoming Outdoor Council for map information and to Erik Molvar for leading field trips in the Red Desert over the years.

Companionship from photography buddies like Mike Conaway and David Halter on many field trips in Adobe Town and afar made things a lot more enjoyable, and sometimes not without excitement. Besides, I need someone to laugh at my jokes sometimes.

Val Brinkerhoff, former photography instructor at WWCC, got me started in photography in 1987, but I never imagined this endeavor would go this far. My experience and know-how in photography are further enhanced from the teaching and advice from great photographers like John Sexton and Anne Larsen.

Thanks to Bill Current, Debora Thaxton Soulé and Ruth Lauritzen for composing flattering letters of references for the grant application. I appreciate the help from Kathy Springmeyer of Sweetgrassbooks for her advice and suggestions for this project.

For years, I have been motivated and inspired by students from my photography classes at Western Wyoming Community College and participants from the BOCES photo workshops.

Finally, I would like to express my love to my wife Betty and our daughter Jessica. Quite often they had to alter dinner plans because I might be still out there photographing. Their patience and support are greatly appreciated.

Paul Ng